THE TEACHER PLEASER

10,000 Instant Activities for the Jewish Classroom

Marji E. Gold-Vukson

Illustrated by
Micheal Gold-Vukson

A.R.E. Publishing, Inc.
Denver, Colorado

Dedication
To Mom and Dad, with love.

Published by:
A.R.E. Publishing, Inc.
Denver, Colorado

Library of Congress Catalog Number 91-70051
ISBN 0-86705-025-X

© A.R.E. Publishing, Inc. 1991

Printed in the United States of America

10 9 8 7 6 5 4 3 2 1

CONTENTS

INTRODUCTION

Consider broccoli. Broccoli is loaded with vitamin A and beta-carotene, contains a nice amount of calcium (as veggies go), and is billed as an all-around super vegetable. But, what possible good can that lovely broccoli do if your kids are resistant to eating it? The trick is to get the broccoli into the kids. The miracle is to get the kids to want to eat the broccoli.

Sure, lots of things are good for kids. Take, for instance, your curriculum. Your curriculum is packed with good things for them. You have all kinds of objectives (both cognitive and affective) that you want your students to master. (It's good for them!) But, as wonderful and necessary as your curriculum is, if your students resist it, what have you accomplished?

The Teacher Pleaser has been designed to inspire your students to want to learn the material that you are presenting to them. The activities here are enticing. You will find them to be engaging and exciting. Moreover, they are designed to be intrinsically motivating, to cause the students to seek out and welcome opportunities for research and learning.

About This Book

The Teacher Pleaser is easy to use. Begin by selecting one of the worksheets (any page from 1-67). The worksheet you pick will determine the type of project your students will do. The 32 worksheets are divided into three categories: 1) Individual Activities: Pencil, Marker, and Paper Activities (pages 1-29); 2) Individual Activities: Hands-on Activity Starters (pages 33-43); and 3) Partner and Group Activities (pages 47-67). Choose one of the worksheets to reproduce for your class. (The pages are perforated for easy removal from the book.)

Now, locate a desired curriculum area — history, holidays, prayers, symbols, etc. (Curriculum Areas on pages 70-90). Choose a topic from the list (or, make up one of your own). Using a black felt-tip pen, write the topic in the appropriate area on the worksheet or on a photocopy of the worksheet.

Finally, photocopy worksheets for your class. Be sure to instruct students to write their names (and the date, if desired) on their worksheets.

There are over 10,000 possible activity/topic combinations presented here. In almost every case, any activity starter can be used with any suggested topic. A "Grid of Combinations" is opposite each curriculum area. These grids will allow you to double check for the appropriateness of the particular activity/topic combinations for each of the "individual activities." (Because all of the "Partner and Group Activities" combinations work well together, grids have not been included for any of them.)

To use the grid, locate the title of your worksheet (e.g., "Hold the Presses") in the column at the left of the grid. You will notice a numeral to the right of the title. This number describes exactly how many specific activity choices are presented under that title. In the case of "Hold the Presses," there are two possible choices. Your students may either 1) compose a magazine article or 2) compose a newspaper editorial.

Next, locate the row of numerals across the top of the grid. Find the numeral which correlates with the specific topic you have selected. For instance, if you were doing a unit on Israel and wanted your class to write about agriculture in Israel, number 17 under the Curriculum Area of "Israel" would meet your needs. The exact combination you have chosen, therefore, would read, "Compose a magazine article or newspaper editorial in which you make a prediction about agriculture in Israel." Is this an appropriate combination? Look at the space on the grid where the title "Hold the Presses" and the number 17 intersect. A circle (○) in the space indicates an excellent combination.

Notice that the intersection of "Hold the Presses" and number 22 does not yield a circle. Instead, a diamond (◆) appears. This is because the combination ("Compose a magazine article or newspaper editorial in which you make a prediction about what it might have been like to be a member of the Haganah in 1948") needs some minor rewording to correct for tense. (It would be difficult to make a *prediction* about something that happened in the past.) So, a diamond indicates a good combination, but one that may require minor rewording.

A star (✱) in the space indicates that, for a particular item, teacher discretion is recommended. Stars are quite rare, and none appear on the grid where the worksheet "Hold the Presses" and the curriculum area of Israel intersect.

Because there are 51 different products (mask, mobile, riddle, skit, etc.) associated with the worksheets in this book, it is possible that your students will need assistance with some of them. Guide the students to the appropriate outside resources.

The Teacher Pleaser is a multi-purpose tool which can be tailored to your program in a variety of ways. Are you looking for exciting components for your learning centers? Are there times when meaningful seat work is required? You will probably find that pages included in the section called "Individual Activities: Pencil, Marker, and Paper Activities" are ideally suited to meet both

of these needs. To provide your students with excellent enrichment projects which can be completed either at school or at home (a real bonus if parent involvement is desired), be sure to check the projects presented under "Individual Activities: Hands-on Activity Starters." For whole class culminating experiences, the "Partner and Group Activities" are tops!

Remember, *The Teacher Pleaser* is a book of ideas. You are welcome to enhance the activities by providing your students with additional supplies and materials (e.g., extra paper for longer compositions, interesting art supplies). You are never limited to the suggestions offered here, and space has been provided within every "Curriculum Area" for your own topics. In addition, "Beyond 10,000" (page 69) has been included in case you want to create your own unique activities. There is even a Glossary of all of the underlined words in the text and "extension" exercises for those of your students who want to elaborate upon their projects!

Have fun with *The Teacher Pleaser*. Oh, and pass the broccoli, please.

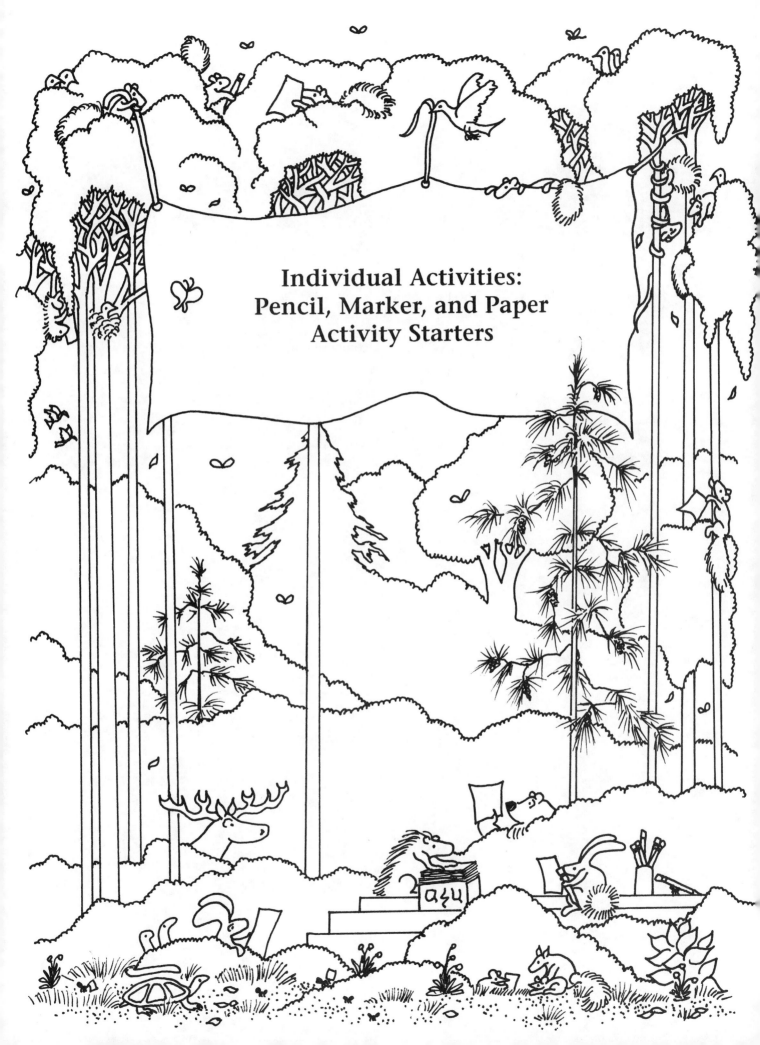

Individual Activities:
Pencil, Marker, and Paper
Activity Starters

And I Quote

Coin a catchy phrase or slogan referring to

Attention, Please

Prepare a public service announcement informing people about the positive aspects (or warning people about the negative aspects) of

Dear Diary

Keep a journal, log, or diary for a week, showing that you know, first hand, a lot about

Copy an interesting passage to here from your journal, log, or diary:

Extension:

Your journal might make an interesting and enjoyable booklet.
Consider placing your completed journal in a classroom
library so that others may read it.

5

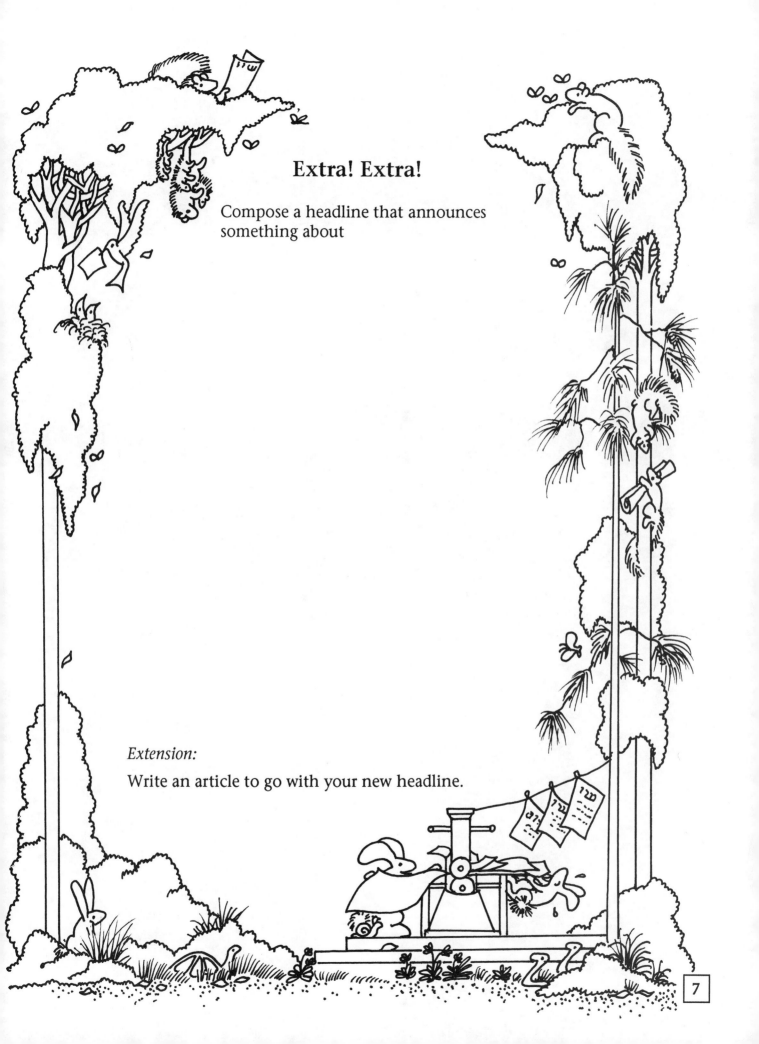

Extra! Extra!

Compose a headline that announces
something about

Extension:

Write an article to go with your new headline.

7

Haiku! (Gesundheit!)

Write a haiku (or a poem in any other form) concerning

Hold the Presses!

Compose a magazine article or newspaper editorial in which you make a prediction about

Extension:

Consider submitting your article or editorial to a publisher. Ask your local librarian for an up-to-date list of magazines that publish articles by students.

In the Name of the Law

Propose a new law concerning

Extension:

Discuss (or debate) your proposed
new law with your classmates.

It's a Date

Design a calendar page with entries reflecting something about

FOREST DAY

MEADOW DAY

Once Upon a Time

Write a short story (or, at least one chapter in a book about)

Title:

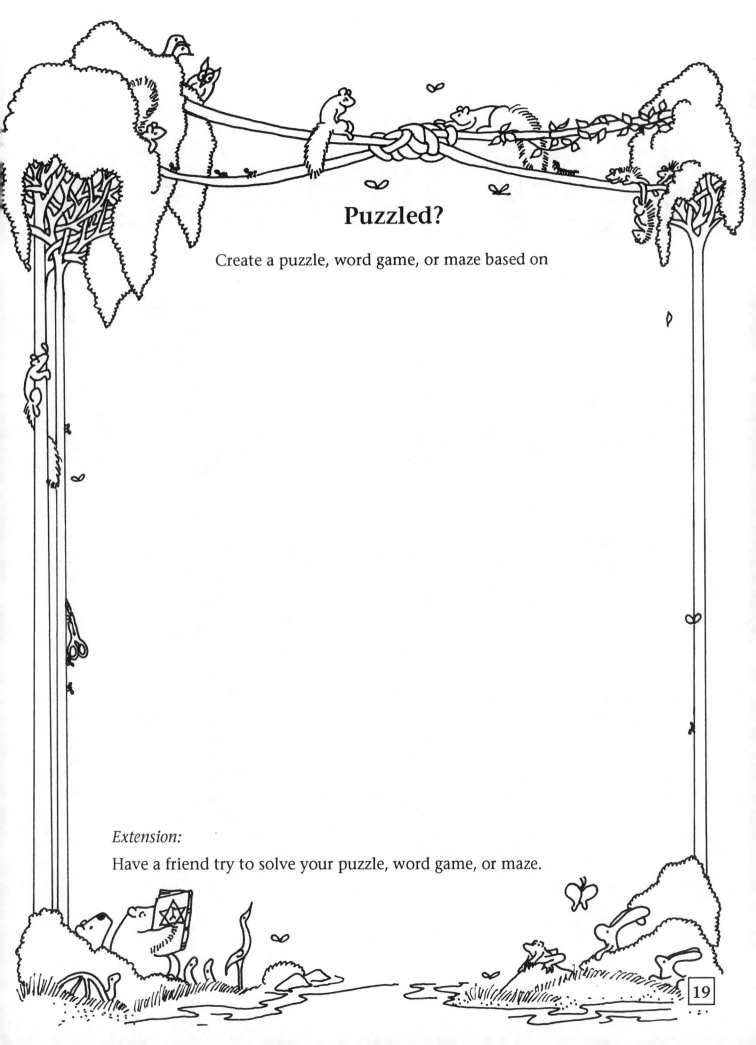

Puzzled?

Create a puzzle, word game, or maze based on

Extension:

Have a friend try to solve your puzzle, word game, or maze.

Rags to Stitches

Design a quilt panel which details or represents something about

Extensions:

1. Combine your unique panel with the panels of others in your class to form a whole quilt. This might make an attractive bulletin board display.

2. Stitch an actual quilt panel based on your design.

Study Up!

Outline a study, experiment, or research project dealing with

Extension:

Carry out your study or experiment. Share the results with your class.

Tongue-Tied

Compose a riddle, joke, tongue twister, or limerick
which involves

Extension:

Try your riddle, joke, tongue twister, or limerick on a friend.

Treble Trouble

Compose the music and/or words for a song about

Title of Song:

Very Funny!

Draw a cartoon or comic strip which expresses a
humorous or cynical view of

Individual Activities:
Hands-on Activity Starters

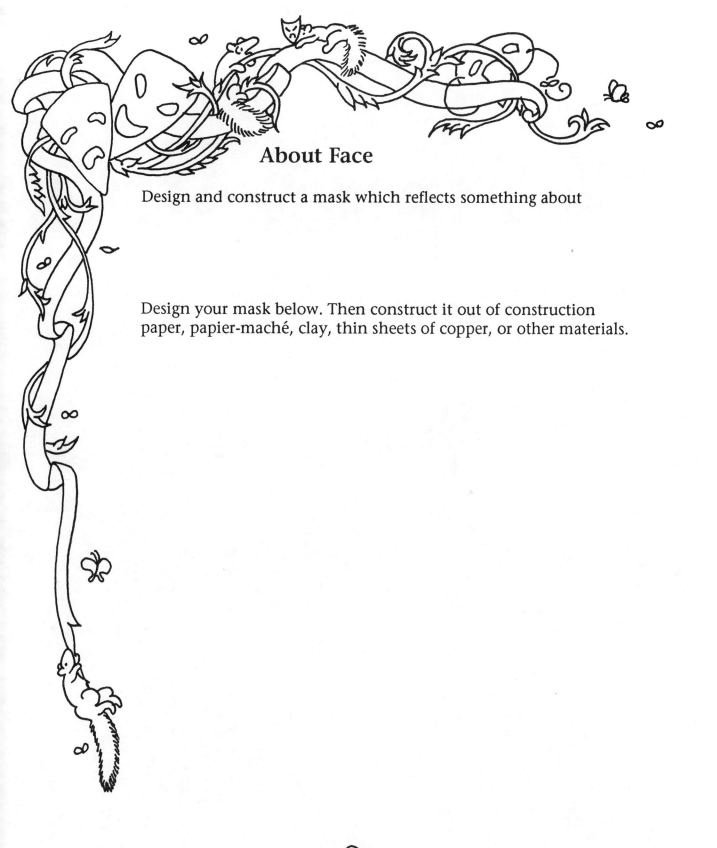

About Face

Design and construct a mask which reflects something about

Design your mask below. Then construct it out of construction paper, papier-maché, clay, thin sheets of copper, or other materials.

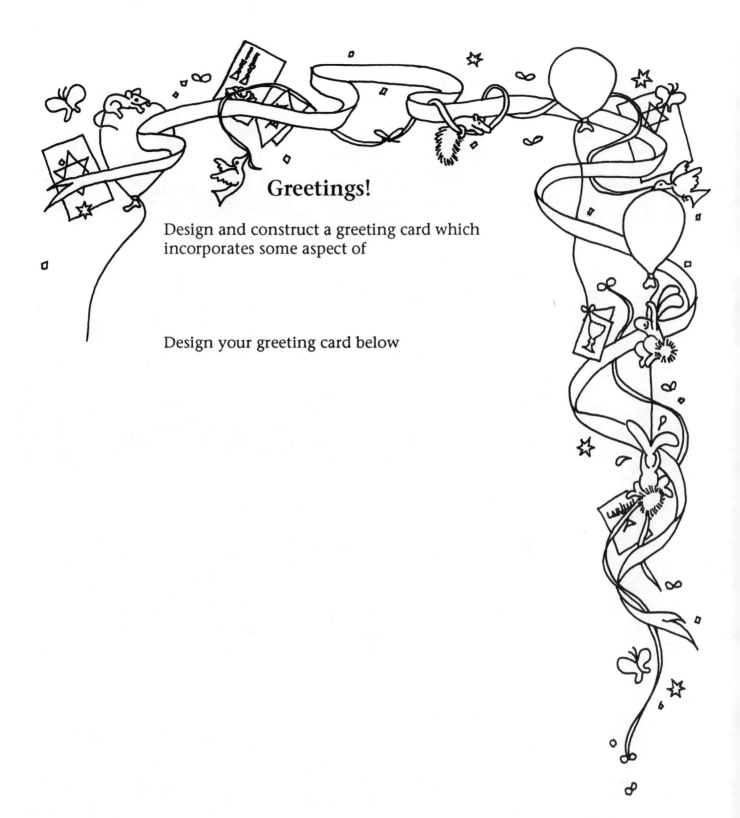

Greetings!

Design and construct a greeting card which incorporates some aspect of

Design your greeting card below

Extension:

It might be fun to try an interesting printing technique
in the creation of your card, too.

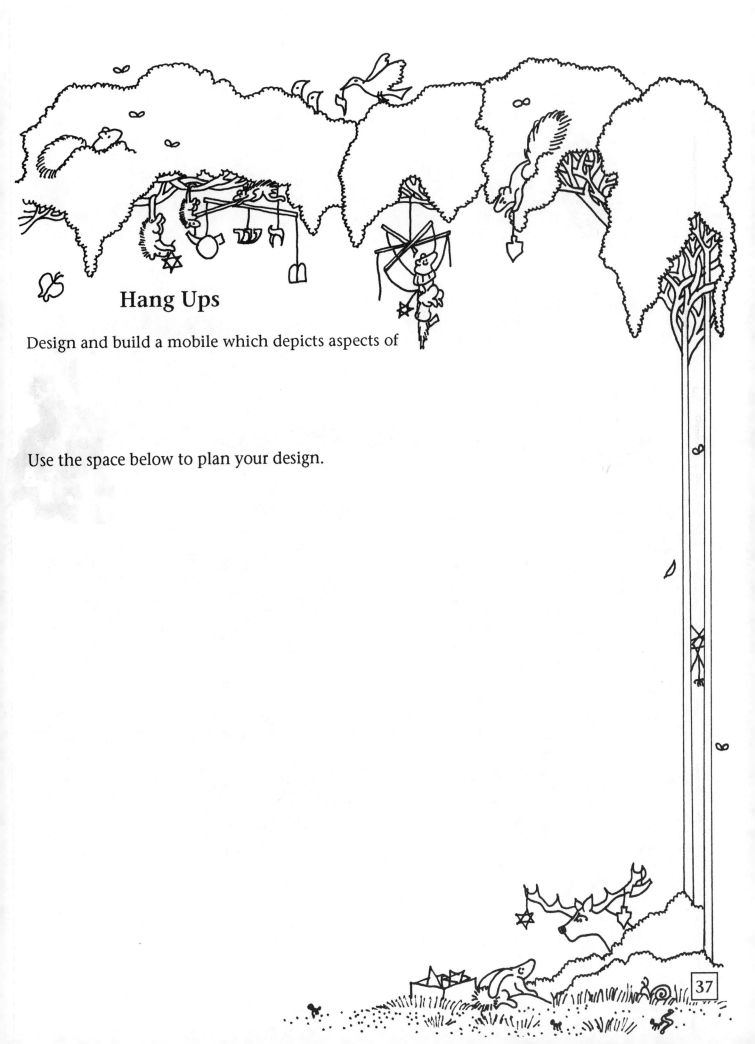

Hang Ups

Design and build a mobile which depicts aspects of

Use the space below to plan your design.

Hats Off to You

Design and construct a hat inspired by

Use felt, cardboard, woven paper, stiff fabric, and/or straw in the construction of your hat.

Papier Trained

Build a papier-maché sculpture which shows (or represents) something about

In this space, include any sketches, diagrams, notes, etc.

Say "Cheese"

Take a photograph which, in some way, shows
something about

In this space, jot down notes as you think through this assignment.
What will you photograph? How will the photo depict your subject?

43

Partner and Group
Activities

Exit, Stage Left

With your partner or group, prepare and perform a skit
which demonstrates something about

Write your script, stage directions, etc., here.
Use additional paper as necessary.

Title of skit:

For the Record

With your partner or group, prepare for an interview with an an expert who knows a great deal about

Write your interview questions (and related notes) here:

Extension:

Conduct an interview using your questions.

Give Me a Hand

With your partner or group, create a puppet show or flannel board story which illustrates something about

Write your script and any stage directions here:

Extension:

Produce your show.

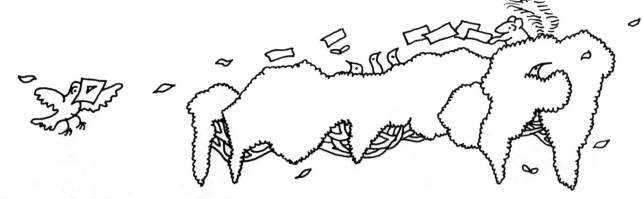

Information, Please

With your partner or group, create a three-dimensional display
to inform others about

In this space, include diagrams, notes, etc.

53

Picture It

With your partner or group, design a mural, banner, or diorama which depicts something about

Extension:

Create your mural, banner, or diorama.

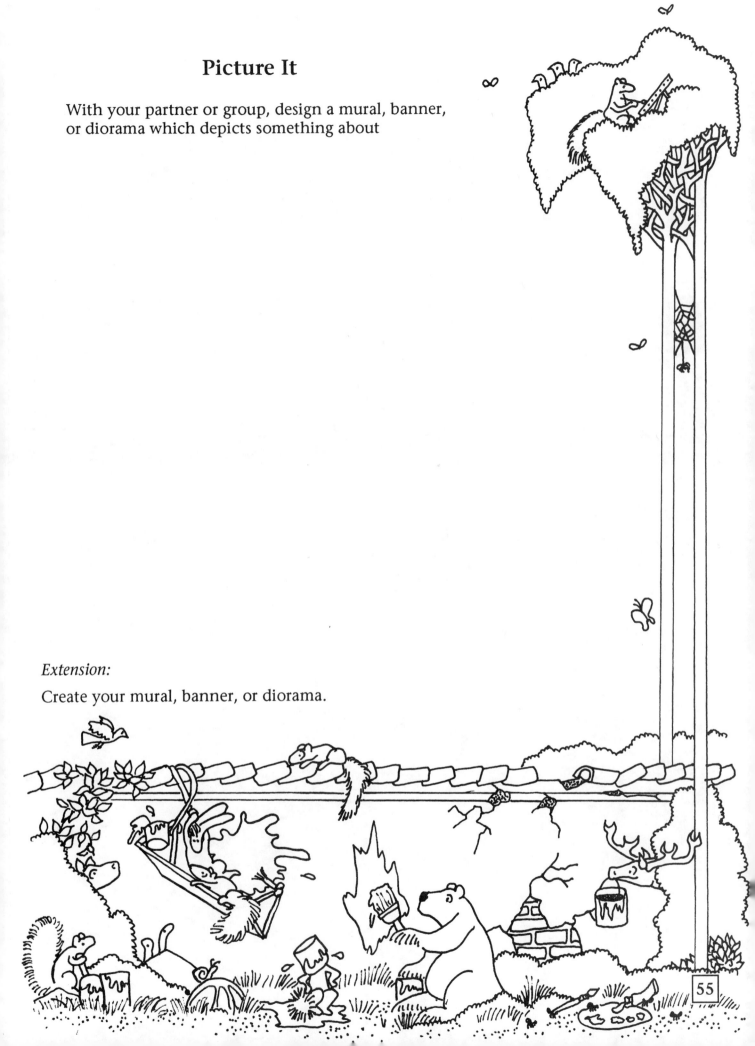

55

Please Stay Tuned

With your partner or group, write and produce a radio play or an audio tape about

In this space, include your script, notes about sound effects, etc.

Quiet, Please!

With your partner or group, pantomime something about

In this space, include notes, diagrams, stage directions, etc.

Extension:

When your pantomime routine is perfected,
present it to your class.

That's a Take

With your partner or group, outline a script for a video or an audio tape which shows aspects of

In this space, write your script, notes, stage directions, etc.

Extension:

Produce your video or audiotape.

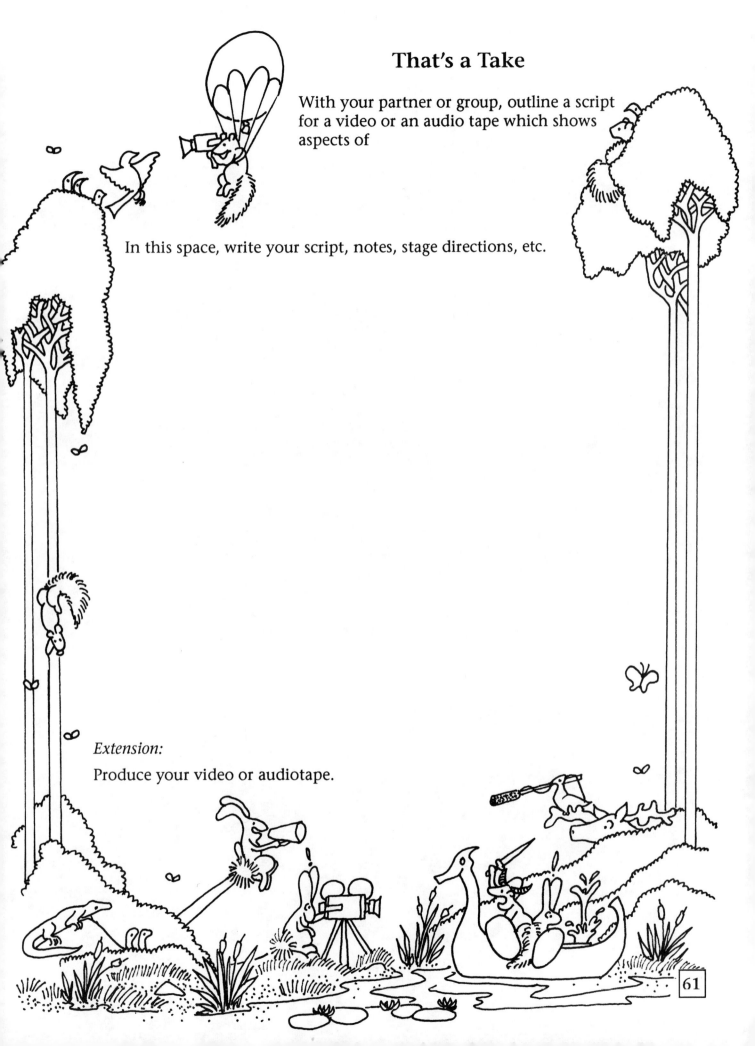

That's Debatable

With your partner or group, plan for a debate concerning something about

In this space, outline your debate. Include notes about teams, rules, reference materials, etc.

Extension:

Debate the issue with other students.

The Old Soft Shoe

With your partner or group, choreograph a dance which communicates something about

In this space, write your notes, diagrams, etc.

Extension:

Perform your dance.

65

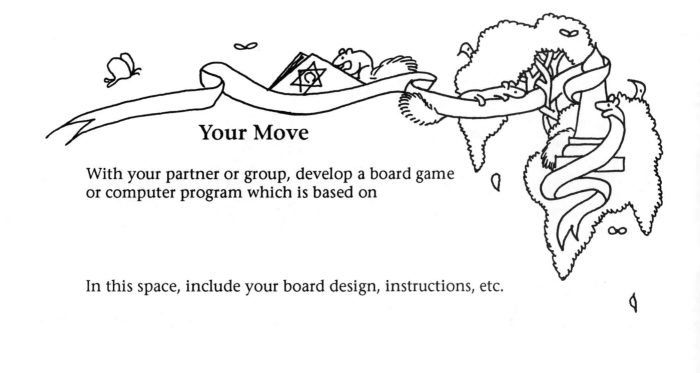

Your Move

With your partner or group, develop a board game or computer program which is based on

In this space, include your board design, instructions, etc.

Extension:

Make a game based on your design and play it with your classmates.

Curriculum Areas

CURRICULUM AREA: COMPARATIVE JUDAISM

Suggested Topics:

1. The Chabad Lubavitch.

2. The Hasidic movement.

3. Orthodox Judaism.

4. Conservative Judaism.

5. Reconstructionist Judaism.

6. The Reform movement.

7. Progressive or liberal Judaism.

8. Secular Judaism.

9. At least three theological beliefs shared by most Jews.

10. A day in the life of a Hasidic family.

11. A conversation about life-styles between a Hasidic girl and her Reform friend.

12. The role of women in an Orthodox synagogue.

13. The role of women in a Reform or Reconstructionist synagogue.

14. The observations of a non-Orthodox child visiting an Orthodox service for the first time.

15. The similarities and differences between Reform, Conservative, and Orthodox synagogues and sanctuaries.

16. The similarities and differences between Reform, Conservative, and Orthodox services (leaders, music, prayerbooks, atmosphere, etc.).

17. The history and development of one or more branches of Judaism.

18. The good points about the fact that there are many branches of Judaism.

19. The bad points about the fact that there are many branches of Judaism.

20. Other:

Individual Activities:
Pencil, Marker, & Paper Activity Starters

	1	2	3	4	5	6	7	8	9	10	11	12	13	14	15	16	17	18	19	20	21
And I Quote (2)	o	o	o	o	o	o	o	o	o	o	o	o	o	o	o	o	o	o	o	o	
Attention, Please (1)	o	o	o	o	o	o	o	o	o	o	o	o	o	o	o	o	o	o	o	o	
Dear Diary (3)	o	o	o	o	o	o	o	o	o	o	o	o	o	o	o	o	o	o	o	o	
Extra! Extra! (1)	o	o	o	o	o	o	o	o	o	o	o	o	o	o	o	o	o	o	o	o	
Haiku! (Gesundheit!) (1)	o	o	o	o	o	o	o	o	o	o	o	o	o	o	o	o	o	o	o	o	
Hold the Presses (2)	o	o	o	o	o	o	o	o	o	o	o	o	o	o	o	o	o	o	o	o	
In the Name of the Law (1)	o	o	o	o	o	o	o	o	o	o	o	o	o	o	o	o	o	o	o	o	
It's a Date (1)	o	o	o	o	o	o	o	o	o	o	o	o	o	o	o	o	o	o	o	o	
Once Upon a Time (2)	o	o	o	o	o	o	o	o	o	o	o	o	o	o	o	o	o	o	o	o	
Puzzled? (3)	o	o	o	o	o	o	o	o	o	o	o	o	o	o	o	o	o	o	o	o	
Rags to Stitches (1)	o	o	o	o	o	o	o	o	o	o	o	o	o	o	o	o	o	o	o	o	
Study Up! (3)	o	o	o	o	o	o	o	o	o	o	o	o	o	o	o	o	o	o	o	o	
Tongue Tied (4)	o	o	o	o	o	o	o	o	o	o	o	o	o	o	o	o	o	o	o	o	
Treble Trouble (2)	o	o	o	o	o	o	o	o	o	o	o	o	o	o	o	o	o	o	o	o	
Very Funny! (2)	*	*	*	*	*	*	*	*	*	o	o	o	o	o	o	o	o	o	o	o	
Other																					

Individual Activities:
Pencil, Marker, & Paper Activity Starters

	1	2	3	4	5	6	7	8	9	10	11	12	13	14	15	16	17	18	19	20	21
About Face (1)	o	o	o	o	o	o	o	o	o	o	o	o	o	o	o	o	o	o	o	o	
Greetings! (1)	o	o	o	o	o	o	o	o	o	o	o	o	o	o	o	o	o	o	o	o	
Hang Ups (1)	o	o	o	o	o	o	o	o	o	o	o	o	o	o	o	o	o	o	o	o	
Hats Off to You (1)	o	o	o	o	o	o	o	o	o	o	o	o	o	o	o	o	o	o	o	o	
Papier Trained (1)	o	o	o	o	o	o	o	o	o	o	o	o	o	o	o	o	o	o	o	o	
Say "Cheese" (1)	o	o	o	o	o	o	o	o	o	o	o	o	o	o	o	o	o	o	o	o	
Other																					

Partner and Group Activities

All "Partner and Group Activities" combinations work well together; thus, no grid is included.

o   Excellent combination

♦   Good combination (needs minor rewording)

*   Teacher discretion advised

CURRICULUM AREA: ETHICS AND VALUES

Suggested Topics:

1. The influence of Jewish values on the ideas and actions of America's founding mothers and fathers.

2. Several of the biblical events upon which social action is based.

3. The ethical treatment of our planet and environment.

4. Social justice.

5. The humane and responsible treatment of animals.

6. Our responsibilities to other Jews.

7. Our responsibilities to and interactions with people everywhere.

8. Ethics and values in current events.

9. Your own value system.

10. The influences of Judaism on my personal value system.

11. The ways parents teach values to their young.

12. The ways in which *Pirke Avot* (Ethics of the Fathers) relates to modern times.

13. Jewish values of love and marriage.

14. Jewish views of life and death.

15. Ethics in medicine.

16. Ethics in business.

17. Anti-Semitism.

18. Tzedakah.

19. Other:

Individual Activities:
Pencil, Marker, & Paper Activity Starters

	1	2	3	4	5	6	7	8	9	10	11	12	13	14	15	16	17	18	19	20
And I Quote (2)	○	○	○	○	○	○	○	○	○	○	○	○	○	○	○	○	○	○	○	○
Attention, Please (1)	○	○	○	○	○	○	○	○	○	○	○	○	○	○	○	○	○	○	○	○
Dear Diary (3)	○	○	○	○	○	○	○	○	○	○	○	○	○	○	○	○	○	○	○	○
Extra! Extra! (1)	○	○	○	○	○	○	○	○	○	○	○	○	○	○	○	○	○	○	○	○
Haiku! (Gesundheit!) (1)	○	○	○	○	○	○	○	○	○	○	○	○	○	○	○	○	○	○	○	○
Hold the Presses (2)	◆	◆	○	○	○	○	○	○	○	○	◆	◆	○	○	○	○	○	○	○	○
In the Name of the Law (1)	○	○	○	○	○	○	○	○	○	*	○	○	*	*	○	○	◆	◆	○	○
It's a Date (1)	○	○	○	○	○	○	○	○	○	○	○	○	○	○	○	○	○	○	○	○
Once Upon a Time (2)	○	○	○	○	○	○	○	○	○	○	○	○	○	○	○	○	○	○	○	○
Puzzled? (3)	○	○	○	○	○	○	○	○	○	○	○	○	○	○	○	○	○	○	○	○
Rags to Stitches (1)	○	○	○	○	○	○	○	○	○	○	○	○	○	○	○	○	○	○	○	○
Study Up! (3)	○	○	○	○	○	○	○	○	○	○	○	○	○	○	○	○	○	○	○	○
Tongue Tied (4)	○	○	○	○	○	○	○	○	○	○	○	○	○	○	○	○	○	○	○	○
Treble Trouble (2)	○	○	○	○	○	○	○	○	○	○	○	○	○	○	○	○	○	○	○	○
Very Funny! (2)	○	○	○	○	○	○	○	○	○	○	○	○	○	○	○	○	*	○	○	
Other																				

Individual Activities:
Pencil, Marker, & Paper Activity Starters

	1	2	3	4	5	6	7	8	9	10	11	12	13	14	15	16	17	18	19	20
About Face (1)	○	○	○	○	○	○	○	○	○	○	○	○	○	○	○	○	○	○	○	○
Greetings! (1)	○	○	○	○	○	○	○	○	○	○	○	○	○	○	○	○	*	○	○	○
Hang Ups (1)	○	○	○	○	○	○	○	○	○	○	○	○	○	○	○	○	○	○	○	○
Hats Off to You (1)	○	○	○	○	○	○	○	○	○	○	○	○	○	○	○	○	○	○	○	○
Papier Trained (1)	○	○	○	○	○	○	○	○	○	○	○	○	○	○	○	○	○	○	○	○
Say "Cheese" (1)	○	○	○	○	○	○	○	○	○	○	○	○	○	○	○	○	○	○	○	○
Other																				

Partner and Group Activities

All "Partner and Group Activities" combinations work well together; thus, no grid is included.

- ○ Excellent combination
- ◆ Good combination (needs minor rewording)
- * Teacher discretion advised

CURRICULUM AREA: GOD

Suggested Topics:

1. God.

2. Your own questions about God.

3. A discussion about God between an observant Jewish child and an observant non-Jewish child.

4. A discussion about God between a Jew and an atheist.

5. Traditional Jewish views of God.

6. The covenant between God and Abraham.

7. Indications that we are created in "God's image."

8. How God helps us and how we help God.

9. The many names of God.

10. Evidence of God in our world.

11. The portrayal of God in literature, music, and/or art.

12. A "conversation" with God.

13. A very young child's ideas about God.

14. The importance of God.

15. Various ways to communicate with God.

16. Things that have been done "in the name of God."

17. Your Rabbi's (or another Rabbi or Jewish scholar's) ideas about God.

18. How God may "feel" about current world events (based on what the Bible says God felt about similar past events).

19. Other:

Individual Activities:
Pencil, Marker, & Paper Activity Starters

	1	2	3	4	5	6	7	8	9	10	11	12	13	14	15	16	17	18	19	20
And I Quote (2)	○	○	○	○	○	○	○	○	○	○	○	○	○	○	○	○	○	○	○	
Attention, Please (1)	○	○	○	○	○	○	○	○	○	○	○	○	○	○	○	○	○	○	○	
Dear Diary (3)	○	○	○	○	○	○	○	○	○	○	○	○	○	○	○	○	○	○	○	
Extra! Extra! (1)	○	○	○	○	○	○	○	○	○	○	○	○	○	○	○	○	○	○	○	
Haiku! (Gesundheit!) (1)	○	○	○	○	○	○	○	○	○	○	○	○	○	○	○	○	○	○	○	
Hold the Presses (2)	○	○	○	○	○	○	○	○	○	○	○	○	○	○	○	◆	○	○	○	
In the Name of the Law (1)	*	○	○	○	○	○	○	○	○	○	○	○	○	○	○	○	○	○	○	
It's a Date (1)	○	○	○	○	○	○	○	○	○	○	○	○	○	○	○	○	○	○	○	
Once Upon a Time (2)	○	○	○	○	○	○	○	○	○	○	○	○	○	○	○	○	○	○	○	
Puzzled? (3)	○	○	○	○	○	○	○	○	○	○	○	○	○	○	○	○	○	○	○	
Rags to Stitches (1)	○	○	○	○	○	○	○	○	○	○	○	○	○	○	○	○	○	○	○	
Study Up! (3)	○	○	○	○	○	○	○	○	○	○	○	○	○	○	○	○	○	○	○	
Tongue Tied (4)	○	○	○	○	○	○	○	○	○	○	○	○	○	○	○	○	○	○	○	
Treble Trouble (2)	○	○	○	○	○	○	○	○	○	○	○	○	○	○	○	○	○	○	○	
Very Funny! (2)	*	○	○	○	◆	*	○	○	○	○	○	○	○	○	○	○	○	○	○	
Other																				

Individual Activities:
Pencil, Marker, & Paper Activity Starters

	1	2	3	4	5	6	7	8	9	10	11	12	13	14	15	16	17	18	19	20
About Face (1)	○	○	○	○	○	○	○	○	○	○	○	○	○	○	○	○	○	○	○	
Greetings! (1)	○	○	○	○	○	○	○	○	○	○	○	○	○	○	○	○	○	○	○	
Hang Ups (1)	○	○	○	○	○	○	○	○	○	○	○	○	○	○	○	○	○	○	○	
Hats Off to You (1)	◆	○	○	○	○	○	○	○	○	○	○	○	○	○	○	○	○	○	○	
Papier Trained (1)	○	○	○	○	○	○	○	○	○	○	○	○	○	○	○	○	○	○	○	
Say "Cheese" (1)	○	○	○	○	○	○	○	○	○	○	○	○	○	○	○	○	○	○	○	
Other																				

Partner and Group Activities

All "Partner and Group Activities" combinations work well together; thus, no grid is included.

○ Excellent combination

◆ Good combination (needs minor rewording)

* Teacher discretion advised

CURRICULUM AREA: HEBREW AND YIDDISH

Suggested Topics:

1. The day that Noah, Channan, and Gabriel decided to keep a secret from their buddies . . . and used Hebrew to do it!

2. *Mama-loshen.*

3. Hebrew words associated with prayer.

4. Hebrew words associated with the holiday of _____.

5. The roots and history of the Hebrew language.

6. One child's wacky experiences at Hebrew school.

7. Some Yiddish words that are now popular in mainstream America.

8. Hebrew as an important part of our culture and tradition.

9. Hebrew and Yiddish media (periodicals, etc.) currently available in the United States.

10. Yiddish theater.

11. Other:

Individual Activities:
Pencil, Marker, & Paper Activity Starters

	1	2	3	4	5	6	7	8	9	10	11	12
And I Quote (2)	○	○	○	○	○	○	○	○	○	○	○	
Attention, Please (1)	○	○	○	○	○	○	○	○	○	○	○	
Dear Diary (3)	○	○	○	○	○	○	○	○	○	○	○	
Extra! Extra! (1)	○	○	○	○	○	○	○	○	○	○	○	
Haiku! (Gesundheit!) (1)	○	○	○	○	○	○	○	○	○	○	○	
Hold the Presses (2)	○	○	○	○	○	○	○	○	○	○	○	
In the Name of the Law (1)	○	○	○	○	○	○	○	○	○	○	○	
It's a Date (1)	○	○	○	○	○	○	○	○	○	○	○	
Once Upon a Time (2)	○	○	○	○	○	○	○	○	○	○	○	
Puzzled? (3)	○	○	○	○	○	○	○	○	○	○	○	
Rags to Stitches (1)	○	○	○	○	○	○	○	○	○	○	○	
Study Up! (3)	◆	○	○	○	○	○	○	○	○	○	○	
Tongue Tied (4)	○	○	*	○	○	○	○	○	○	○	○	
Treble Trouble (2)	○	○	○	○	○	○	○	○	○	○	○	
Very Funny! (2)	○	○	*	*	○	○	○	○	○	○	○	
Other												

Individual Activities:
Pencil, Marker, & Paper Activity Starters

	1	2	3	4	5	6	7	8	9	10	11	12
About Face (1)	○	○	○	○	○	○	○	○	○	○	○	
Greetings! (1)	○	○	○	○	○	○	○	○	○	○	○	
Hang Ups (1)	○	○	○	○	○	○	○	○	○	○	○	
Hats Off to You (1)	○	○	○	○	○	○	○	○	○	○	○	
Papier Trained (1)	○	○	○	○	○	○	○	○	○	○	○	
Say "Cheese" (1)	○	○	○	○	○	○	○	○	○	○	○	
Other												

Partner and Group Activities

All "Partner and Group Activities" combinations work well together; thus, no grid is included.

○ Excellent combination
◆ Good combination (needs minor rewording)
* Teacher discretion advised

CURRICULUM AREA: HISTORY AND PERSONALITIES

Suggested Topics:

1. The travels of Abraham and Sarah from Ur to the <u>Land of Canaan</u> in about 1800 B.C.E.
2. Joseph's experiences in Egypt during the years of famine in around 1650 B.C.E.
3. The years of slavery under the Pharaohs of Egypt.
4. What it may have been like to wander with Moses through the desert from Egypt to the Land of Israel in about 1200 B.C.E.
5. A conversation between Saul and David, the first and second kings of Israel.
6. An interview with the wise King Solomon.
7. What it may have been like to have been an architect of the Holy Temple in Jerusalem.
8. The splitting of the kingdom into Israel (Samaria) and Judah (Judea) in about 925 B.C.E.
9. The conquering of Israel and the capture of her people by the Assyrians in about 721 B.C.E.
10. The conquering of Judea and the destruction of the Holy Temple by the Babylonians in about 586 B.C.E.
11. The Hellenization (imposing Greek culture on the people) of Judea in around 200 B.C.E.
12. The revolt against the Greek-Syrian King, Antiochus, by Judah Maccabee and his small army in around 168 B.C.E.
13. An announcement of startling "new" information contained in the <u>Dead Sea Scrolls</u>.
14. A meeting of the inhabitants of Masada in about 73 C.E.
15. The feelings of a Jewish family as they are being driven out of Jerusalem (and forbidden to practice Judaism) by the Romans in the year 132 C.E.
16. The thoughts and plans of Rabbi Judah HaNasi as he selected the laws to go into the <u>Mishna</u> in 210 C.E.
17. The completion of the <u>Babylonian Talmud</u> in the year 495 C.E.
18. The spread of Judaism into Russia, Spain, England, France, and Germany in the period from the year 740 to about 1100 C.E.
19. What it was like to study with <u>Rashi</u> and <u>Rabbenu Gershom</u> in around the year 1000 C.E.
20. The ideas presented at a hurried meeting in 1348, when rumors circulated that the Black Plague (which killed thousands of Europeans) was caused by Jews who had poisoned the wells.
21. The hopes of a <u>Marrano</u> family in 1492.
22. What it might have been like to be in on the birth of the <u>Hasidic movement</u> in the 1750s.
23. The plans of the first Zionists, who bought land from the Arabs and settled in Palestine in 1881.
24. What it was like to be a leader of the First Zionist Congress in 1897.
25. What it might have been like to be the first journalist to read the <u>Balfour Declaration</u> in 1917.
26. The relationship between <u>Chaim Weizmann</u>, <u>David Ben-Gurion</u>, and <u>Golda Meir</u>.
27. The establishment of the State of Israel in 1948.
28. The thoughts and feelings of Anne Frank.
29. The thoughts of a young soldier during the Six Day War of 1967.
30. Major changes occurring within American Jewish life today.
31. Being Jewish in the twenty-first century.
32. Other:

Individual Activities:
Pencil, Marker, & Paper Activity Starters

	1	2	3	4	5	6	7	8	9	10	11	12	13	14	15	16	17	18	19	20	21	22	23	24	25	26	27	28	29	30	31	32	33
And I Quote (2)	○	○	○	○	○	○	○	○	○	○	○	○	○	○	○	○	○	○	○	○	○	○	○	○	○	○	○	*	○	○	○	○	
Attention, Please (1)	○	○	○	○	○	○	○	○	○	○	○	○	○	○	○	○	○	○	○	○	○	○	○	○	○	○	○	○	○	○	○	○	
Dear Diary (3)	○	○	○	○	○	○	○	○	○	○	○	○	○	○	○	○	○	○	○	○	○	○	○	○	○	○	○	○	○	○	○	○	
Extra! Extra! (1)	○	○	○	○	○	○	○	○	○	○	○	○	○	○	○	○	○	○	○	○	○	○	○	○	○	○	○	○	○	○	○	○	
Haiku! (Gesundheit!) (1)	○	○	○	○	○	○	○	○	○	○	○	○	○	○	○	○	○	○	○	○	○	○	○	○	○	○	○	○	○	○	○	○	
Hold the Presses (2)	○	○	○	○	○	○	○	○	○	○	○	○	○	○	○	○	○	○	○	○	○	○	○	○	○	○	○	○	○	○	○	○	
In the Name of the Law (1)	○	○	○	○	○	○	○	○	○	○	○	○	○	○	○	○	○	○	○	○	○	○	○	○	○	○	○	○	○	○	○	○	
It's a Date (1)	○	○	○	○	○	○	○	○	○	○	○	○	○	○	○	○	○	○	○	○	○	○	○	○	○	○	○	○	○	○	○	○	
Once Upon a Time (2)	○	○	○	○	○	○	○	○	○	○	○	○	○	○	○	○	○	○	○	○	○	○	○	○	○	○	○	○	○	○	○	○	
Puzzled? (3)	○	○	○	○	○	○	○	○	○	○	○	○	○	○	○	○	○	○	○	○	○	○	○	○	○	○	○	*	○	○	○	○	
Rags to Stitches (1)	○	○	○	○	○	○	○	○	○	○	○	○	○	○	○	○	○	○	○	○	○	○	○	○	○	○	○	○	○	○	○	○	
Study Up! (3)	○	○	○	○	○	○	○	○	○	○	○	○	○	○	○	○	○	○	○	○	○	○	○	○	○	○	○	○	○	○	○	○	
Tongue Tied (4)	○	○	○	○	○	○	○	○	*	*	*	○	○	*	○	○	○	○	○	○	○	○	○	○	○	○	○	*	○	○	○	○	
Treble Trouble (2)	○	○	○	○	○	○	○	○	○	○	○	○	○	○	○	○	○	○	○	○	○	○	○	○	○	○	○	○	○	○	○	○	
Very Funny! (2)	○	○	○	○	○	○	○	○	*	*	*	○	○	*	*	○	○	○	○	*	○	○	○	○	○	○	○	*	*	○	○	○	
Other																																	

Individual Activities:
Pencil, Marker, & Paper Activity Starters

	1	2	3	4	5	6	7	8	9	10	11	12	13	14	15	16	17	18	19	20	21	22	23	24	25	26	27	28	29	30	31	32	33
About Face (1)	○	○	○	○	○	○	○	○	○	○	○	○	○	○	○	○	○	○	○	○	○	○	○	○	○	○	○	○	○	○	○	○	
Greetings! (1)	○	○	○	○	○	○	○	○	*	*	*	○	○	*	*	○	○	○	○	*	○	○	○	○	○	○	○	*	*	○	○	○	
Hang Ups (1)	○	○	○	○	○	○	○	○	○	○	○	○	○	○	○	○	○	○	○	○	○	○	○	○	○	○	○	○	○	○	○	○	
Hats Off to You (1)	○	○	○	○	○	○	○	○	○	○	○	○	○	○	○	○	○	○	○	○	○	○	○	○	○	○	○	○	○	○	○	○	
Papier Trained (1)	○	○	○	○	○	○	○	○	○	○	○	○	○	○	○	○	○	○	○	○	○	○	○	○	○	○	○	○	○	○	○	○	
Say "Cheese" (1)	○	○	○	○	○	○	○	○	○	○	○	○	○	○	○	○	○	○	○	○	○	○	○	○	○	○	○	○	○	○	○	○	
Other																																	

Partner and Group Activities

All "Partner and Group Activities" combinations work well together; thus, no grid is included.

○ Excellent combination

◆ Good combination (needs minor rewording)

* Teacher discretion advised

CURRICULUM AREA: HOLIDAYS, FESTIVALS, AND CELEBRATIONS

Suggested Topics:

1. Rosh Hashanah.

2. Yom Kippur.

3. Sukkot.

4. Simchat Torah.

5. Chanukah.

6. Tu B'Shevat.

7. Purim.

8. Passover.

9. Lag Ba-Omer.

10. Yom Haatzmaut.

11. Yom Hashoah.

12. Shavuot.

13. Tisha B'Av.

14. Rosh Chodesh.

15. Your most memorable holiday celebration.

16. How one Jewish holiday relates to other Jewish holidays.

17. The similarities and differences in the ways Jews of different countries celebrate the holiday of _____.

18. The origins of the holiday of _____.

19. The laws and traditions surrounding the celebration of the holiday of _____.

20. A holiday recipe.

21. A joyous holiday of your choice.

22. A solemn holiday of your choice.

23. What it might be like if a new, never-before-celebrated Jewish holiday was invented.

24. What it is like to celebrate a holiday that most of the other people in your country do not know much about.

25. What it will be like to prepare your home for the holiday of _____.

26. What it would be like if two Jewish holidays (of your choice) were combined to form one new holiday.

27. The specific prayers and blessings recited on the holiday of _____.

28. The month in the Jewish calendar which is, in your opinion, the most important or significant.

29. Other:

Individual Activities:
Pencil, Marker, & Paper Activity Starters

	1	2	3	4	5	6	7	8	9	10	11	12	13	14	15	16	17	18	19	20	21	22	23	24	25	26	27	28	29	30
And I Quote (2)	○	○	○	○	○	○	○	○	○	○	○	○	○	○	○	○	○	○	○	○	○	○	○	○	○	○	○	○	○	
Attention, Please (1)	○	○	○	○	○	○	○	○	○	○	○	○	○	○	○	○	○	○	○	○	○	○	○	○	○	○	○	○	○	
Dear Diary (3)	○	○	○	○	○	○	○	○	○	○	○	○	○	○	○	○	○	○	○	○	○	○	○	○	○	○	○	○	○	
Extra! Extra! (1)	○	○	○	○	○	○	○	○	○	○	○	○	○	○	○	○	○	○	○	○	○	○	○	○	○	○	○	○	○	
Haiku! (Gesundheit!) (1)	○	○	○	○	○	○	○	○	○	○	○	○	○	○	○	○	○	○	○	○	○	○	○	○	○	○	○	○	○	
Hold the Presses (2)	○	○	○	○	○	○	○	○	○	○	○	○	○	○	◆	◆	◆	◆	○	○	○	○	○	◆	○	○	○	○	○	
In the Name of the Law (1)	○	○	○	○	○	○	○	○	○	○	○	○	○	○	○	○	○	○	○	○	○	○	○	○	○	○	○	○	○	
It's a Date (1)	○	○	○	○	○	○	○	○	○	○	○	○	○	○	○	○	○	○	○	○	○	○	○	○	○	○	○	○	○	
Once Upon a Time (2)	○	○	○	○	○	○	○	○	○	○	○	○	○	○	○	○	○	○	○	○	○	○	○	○	○	○	○	○	○	
Puzzled? (3)	○	○	○	○	○	○	○	○	○	○	○	○	○	○	○	○	○	○	○	○	○	○	○	○	○	○	○	○	○	
Rags to Stitches (1)	○	○	○	○	○	○	○	○	○	○	○	○	○	○	○	○	○	○	○	○	○	○	○	○	○	○	○	○	○	
Study Up! (3)	○	○	○	○	○	○	○	○	○	○	○	○	○	○	○	○	○	○	○	○	○	○	○	○	○	○	○	○	○	
Tongue Tied (4)	○	○	○	○	○	○	○	○	○	○	○	○	○	○	○	○	○	○	○	○	○	*	○	○	○	○	*	○	○	
Treble Trouble (2)	○	○	○	○	○	○	○	○	○	○	○	○	○	○	○	○	○	○	○	○	○	○	○	○	○	○	○	○	○	
Very Funny! (2)	○	○	○	○	○	○	○	○	○	○	○	○	○	○	○	○	○	○	○	○	○	*	○	○	○	○	*	○	○	
Other																														

Individual Activities:
Pencil, Marker, & Paper Activity Starters

	1	2	3	4	5	6	7	8	9	10	11	12	13	14	15	16	17	18	19	20	21	22	23	24	25	26	27	28	29	30
About Face (1)	○	○	○	○	○	○	○	○	○	○	○	○	○	○	○	○	○	○	○	○	○	○	○	○	○	○	○	○	○	
Greetings! (1)	○	○	○	○	○	○	○	○	○	○	○	○	○	○	○	○	○	○	○	○	○	○	○	○	○	○	○	○	○	
Hang Ups (1)	○	○	○	○	○	○	○	○	○	○	○	○	○	○	○	○	○	○	○	○	○	○	○	○	○	○	○	○	○	
Hats Off to You (1)	○	○	○	○	○	○	○	○	○	○	○	○	○	○	○	○	○	○	○	○	○	○	○	○	○	○	○	○	○	
Papier Trained (1)	○	○	○	○	○	○	○	○	○	○	○	○	○	○	○	○	○	○	○	○	○	○	○	○	○	○	○	○	○	
Say "Cheese" (1)	○	○	○	○	○	○	○	○	○	○	○	○	○	○	○	○	○	○	○	○	○	○	○	○	○	○	○	○	○	
Other																														

Partner and Group Activities

All "Partner and Group Activities" combinations work well together; thus, no grid is included.

○ Excellent combination

◆ Good combination (needs minor rewording)

* Teacher discretion advised

CURRICULUM AREA: ISRAEL

Suggested Topics:

1. The ties which link Jews in the <u>Diaspora</u> with Jews in Israel.

2. How life in Israel differs from life in this country.

3 The roles of a <u>kibbutznik</u>.

4. Going to school in Israel.

5. What it would be like to be a member of the <u>Knesset</u> during amajor debate.

6. The relationships between Israeli citizens of different religious, cultural, and/or ethnic backgrounds.

7. What the unique geography of Israel is like.

8. What it might be like to make *aliyah*.

9. The arts in Israel.

10. Industry in Israel.

11. What it might be like if lasting peace broke out in the Middle East.

12. <u>Operation Moses</u> and the <u>Beta Yisrael</u>.

13. A visit to Israel.

14. A trip to the *Kotel*.

15. What it might have been like to have traveled with Abraham and Sarah from Ur to the <u>Land of Canaan</u> about 4000 years ago.

16. What it might be like to participate in an archaeological dig in Israel.

17. Agriculture in Israel.

18. Ancient Israel.

19. The Israeli economy.

20. Your job as a dock worker at Israel's most important port.

21. What it is like to live in a country where Jews are in the majority.

22. What it might have been like to be a member of the <u>Haganah</u> in 1948.

23. The unique flora (plants) and fauna (animals) of Israel.

24. Other:

Individual Activities:
Pencil, Marker, & Paper Activity Starters

	1	2	3	4	5	6	7	8	9	10	11	12	13	14	15	16	17	18	19	20	21	22	23	24	25
And I Quote (2)	○	○	○	○	○	○	○	○	○	○	○	○	○	○	○	○	○	○	○	○	○	○	○	○	
Attention, Please (1)	○	○	○	○	○	○	○	○	○	○	○	○	○	○	○	○	○	○	○	○	○	○	○	○	
Dear Diary (3)	○	○	○	○	○	○	○	○	○	○	○	○	○	○	○	○	○	○	○	○	○	○	○	○	
Extra! Extra! (1)	○	○	○	○	○	○	○	○	○	○	○	○	○	○	○	○	○	○	○	○	○	○	○	○	
Haiku! (Gesundheit!) (1)	○	○	○	○	○	○	○	○	○	○	○	○	○	○	○	○	○	○	○	○	○	○	○	○	
Hold the Presses (2)	○	◆	○	○	○	○	◆	○	○	○	○	○	○	○	◆	○	○	○	○	○	○	◆	○	○	
In the Name of the Law (1)	○	○	○	○	◆	○	○	◆	○	○	○	○	○	○	◆	◆	○	○	○	○	◆	◆	○	○	
It's a Date (1)	○	○	○	○	○	○	○	○	○	○	○	○	○	○	○	○	○	○	○	○	○	○	○	○	
Once Upon a Time (2)	○	○	○	○	○	○	○	○	○	○	○	○	○	○	○	○	○	○	○	○	○	○	○	○	
Puzzled? (3)	○	○	○	○	○	○	○	○	○	○	○	○	○	○	○	○	○	○	○	○	○	○	○	○	
Rags to Stitches (1)	○	○	○	○	○	○	○	○	○	○	○	○	○	○	○	○	○	○	○	○	○	○	○	○	
Study Up! (3)	○	○	○	○	○	○	○	○	○	○	○	○	○	○	○	○	○	○	○	○	○	○	○	○	
Tongue Tied (4)	○	○	○	○	○	○	○	○	○	○	○	○	○	○	○	○	○	○	○	○	○	○	○	○	
Treble Trouble (2)	○	○	○	○	○	○	○	○	○	○	○	○	○	○	○	○	○	○	○	○	○	○	○	○	
Very Funny! (2)	○	○	○	○	○	○	○	○	○	○	○	○	○	*	○	○	○	○	○	○	○	○	○	○	
Other																									

Individual Activities:
Pencil, Marker, & Paper Activity Starters

	1	2	3	4	5	6	7	8	9	10	11	12	13	14	15	16	17	18	19	20	21	22	23	24	25
About Face (1)	○	○	○	○	○	○	○	○	○	○	○	○	○	○	○	○	○	○	○	○	○	○	○	○	
Greetings! (1)	○	○	○	○	○	○	○	○	○	○	○	*	○	○	○	○	○	○	○	○	○	○	○	○	
Hang Ups (1)	○	○	○	○	○	○	○	○	○	○	○	○	○	○	○	○	○	○	○	○	○	○	○	○	
Hats Off to You (1)	○	○	○	○	○	○	○	○	○	○	○	○	○	○	○	○	○	○	○	○	○	○	○	○	
Papier Trained (1)	○	○	○	○	○	○	○	○	○	○	○	○	○	○	○	○	○	○	○	○	○	○	○	○	
Say "Cheese" (1)	○	○	○	○	○	○	○	○	○	○	○	○	○	○	○	○	○	○	○	○	○	○	○	○	
Other																									

Partner and Group Activities

All "Partner and Group Activities" combinations work well together; thus, no grid is included.

○   Excellent combination

◆   Good combination (needs minor rewording)

*   Teacher discretion advised

CURRICULUM AREA: JEWISH LIFETIME EVENTS

Suggested Topics:

1. The thoughts of young parents at their son's <u>Brit Milah</u> (Bris).

2. Your creative interpretation of the "thoughts" of a baby girl during her naming ceremony (<u>Brit Bat</u>, <u>Brit Chayim</u>, or <u>Simchat Ha-bat</u>).

3. A humorous turn of events at a <u>Pidyon Ha-Ben</u>.

4. A child's <u>Consecration</u> ceremony.

5. What it might be like to give a <u>Bat Mitzvah</u> or <u>Bar Mitzvah</u> speech.

6. The feelings of a student at his or her <u>Confirmation</u>.

7. The traditional Jewish wedding ceremony.

8. A <u>Chanukat HaBayit</u> or home blessing ceremony.

9. A creative new ceremony which commemorates an especially significant event in Jewish life (e.g., conversion to Judaism, adoption, the establishment of a Jewish home, honoring the elderly, etc.).

10. The funeral of an elderly Jewish scholar.

11. Other:

Individual Activities:
Pencil, Marker, & Paper Activity Starters

	1	2	3	4	5	6	7	8	9	10	11	12
And I Quote (2)	○	○	○	○	○	○	○	○	○	∗	○	
Attention, Please (1)	○	○	○	○	○	○	○	○	○	∗	○	
Dear Diary (3)	○	○	○	○	○	○	○	○	○	○	○	
Extra! Extra! (1)	○	○	○	○	○	○	○	○	○	○	○	
Haiku! (Gesundheit!) (1)	○	○	○	○	○	○	○	○	○	○	○	
Hold the Presses (2)	○	○	○	○	○	○	○	○	○	○	○	
In the Name of the Law (1)	◆	◆	◆	○	◆	◆	○	○	○	○	○	
It's a Date (1)	○	○	○	○	○	○	○	○	○	○	○	
Once Upon a Time (2)	○	○	○	○	○	○	○	○	○	○	○	
Puzzled? (3)	○	○	○	○	○	○	○	○	○	○	○	
Rags to Stitches (1)	○	○	○	○	○	○	○	○	○	○	○	
Study Up! (3)	○	○	○	○	○	○	○	○	○	○	○	
Tongue Tied (4)	○	○	○	○	○	○	○	○	○	∗	○	
Treble Trouble (2)	○	○	○	○	○	○	○	○	○	○	○	
Very Funny! (2)	○	○	○	○	○	○	○	○	○	∗	○	
Other												

Individual Activities:
Pencil, Marker, & Paper Activity Starters

	1	2	3	4	5	6	7	8	9	10	11	12
About Face (1)	○	○	○	○	○	○	○	○	○	○	○	
Greetings! (1)	○	○	○	○	○	○	○	○	○	∗	○	
Hang Ups (1)	○	○	○	○	○	○	○	○	○	○	○	
Hats Off to You (1)	○	○	○	○	○	○	○	○	○	○	○	
Papier Trained (1)	○	○	○	○	○	○	○	○	○	○	○	
Say "Cheese" (1)	○	○	○	○	○	○	○	○	○	○	○	
Other												

Partner and Group Activities

All "Partner and Group Activities" combinations work well together; thus, no grid is included.

○ Excellent combination

◆ Good combination (needs minor rewording)

∗ Teacher discretion advised

CURRICULUM AREA: PRAYERS AND BLESSINGS

Suggested Topics:

1. A young child's first prayer.
2. The modern version of an ancient prayer.
3. *Kavanah*.
4. Why we pray.
5. A traditional prayer or blessing.
6. A specific prayer or blessing of your choice.
7. A "thank you" prayer.
8. A prayer of praise.
9. A prayer in which you ask for something.
10. The similarities and differences between the traditional prayers of Jews and the prayers of Non-Jews.
11. A Hebrew prayer.
12. What you think is the most important prayer.
13. The Rabbi, Chazzan, or other prayer "leader."
14. Praying as a congregation.
15. The order of a worship service.
16. *Davening*.
17. Liturgy or music in prayer.
18. Candles, *tefillin*, and other items used during prayer.
19. A new prayer.
20. Shuckling, bowing, and other movement during prayer.
21. Other:

Individual Activities:
Pencil, Marker, & Paper Activity Starters

	1	2	3	4	5	6	7	8	9	10	11	12	13	14	15	16	17	18	19	20	21	22
And I Quote (2)	○	○	○	○	○	○	○	○	○	○	○	○	○	○	○	○	○	○	○	○	○	
Attention, Please (1)	○	○	○	○	○	○	○	○	○	○	○	○	○	○	○	○	○	○	○	○	○	
Dear Diary (3)	○	○	○	○	○	○	○	○	○	○	○	○	○	○	○	○	○	○	○	○	○	
Extra! Extra! (1)	○	○	○	○	○	○	○	○	○	○	○	○	○	○	○	○	○	○	○	○	○	
Haiku! (Gesundheit!) (1)	○	○	○	○	○	○	○	○	○	○	○	○	○	○	○	○	○	○	○	○	○	
Hold the Presses (2)	○	○	○	◆	○	○	○	○	○	○	○	○	○	○	○	○	○	○	○	○	○	
In the Name of the Law (1)	○	○	○	○	○	○	○	○	○	○	○	○	○	○	○	○	○	○	○	○	○	
It's a Date (1)	○	○	○	○	○	○	○	○	○	○	○	○	○	○	○	○	○	○	○	○	○	
Once Upon a Time (2)	○	○	○	○	○	○	○	○	○	○	○	○	○	○	○	○	○	○	○	○	○	
Puzzled? (3)	○	○	○	○	○	○	○	○	○	○	○	○	○	○	○	○	○	○	○	○	○	
Rags to Stitches (1)	○	○	○	○	○	○	○	○	○	○	○	○	○	○	○	○	○	○	○	○	○	
Study Up! (3)	○	○	○	○	○	○	○	○	○	○	○	○	○	○	○	○	○	○	○	○	○	
Tongue Tied (4)	○	○	○	○	○	○	○	○	○	○	○	○	○	○	○	○	○	○	○	○	○	
Treble Trouble (2)	○	○	○	○	○	○	○	○	○	○	○	○	○	○	○	○	○	○	○	○	○	
Very Funny! (2)	○	*	*	○	*	*	*	*	*	*	*	○	○	○	○	○	○	○	○	○	○	
Other																						

Individual Activities:
Pencil, Marker, & Paper Activity Starters

	1	2	3	4	5	6	7	8	9	10	11	12	13	14	15	16	17	18	19	20	21	22
About Face (1)	○	○	○	○	○	○	○	○	○	○	○	○	○	○	○	○	○	○	○	○	○	
Greetings! (1)	○	○	○	○	○	○	○	○	○	*	○	○	○	○	○	○	○	○	○	○	○	
Hang Ups (1)	○	○	○	○	○	○	○	○	○	○	○	○	○	○	○	○	○	○	○	○	○	
Hats Off to You (1)	○	○	○	○	○	○	○	○	○	○	○	○	○	○	○	○	○	○	○	○	○	
Papier Trained (1)	○	○	○	○	○	○	○	○	○	○	○	○	○	○	○	○	○	○	○	○	○	
Say "Cheese" (1)	○	○	○	○	○	○	○	○	○	○	○	○	○	○	○	○	○	○	○	○	○	
Other																						

Partner and Group Activities

All "Partner and Group Activities" combinations work well together; thus, no grid is included.

○ Excellent combination

◆ Good combination (needs minor rewording)

* Teacher discretion advised

CURRICULUM AREA: JEWISH SYMBOLS AND CEREMONIAL OBJECTS

Suggested Topics:

1. A young child's awe at the mystique of the *Ner Tamid* (Eternal Light).
2. The significance of the Sabbath candles.
3. The explanation for the *challah* cover.
4. A teen-ager's first attempt at putting on *tefillin*.
5. A hidden Torah.
6. The process of creating a shofar.
7. A magical night in the sukkah.
8. An incompatible *lulav* and *etrog.*
9. A unique Simchat Torah flag.
10. A modern day miracle involving a *menorah.*
11. The *Megillat Esther.*
12. The case of the silent *gragger.*
13. An heirloom Seder plate.
14. A missing *Magen David.*
15. A stingy *tzedakah* box.
16. The *mezzuzah* mystery.
17. A *yahrzeit* candle.
18. A *mizrach* that wouldn't stay put.
19. Grandma's prayerbook.
20. A Jewish symbol or ceremonial object of your choice.
21. Other:

Grid of Combinations: Jewish Symbols and Ceremonial Objects

Individual Activities:
Pencil, Marker, & Paper Activity Starters

	1	2	3	4	5	6	7	8	9	10	11	12	13	14	15	16	17	18	19	20	21	22
And I Quote (2)	O	O	O	O	O	O	O	O	O	O	O	O	O	O	O	O	*	O	O	O	O	
Attention, Please (1)	O	O	O	O	O	O	O	O	O	O	O	O	O	O	O	O	O	O	O	O	O	
Dear Diary (3)	O	O	O	O	O	O	O	O	O	O	O	O	O	O	O	O	O	O	O	O	O	
Extra! Extra! (1)	O	O	O	O	O	O	O	O	O	O	O	O	O	O	O	O	O	O	O	O	O	
Haiku! (Gesundheit!) (1)	O	O	O	O	O	O	O	O	O	O	O	O	O	O	O	O	O	O	O	O	O	
Hold the Presses (2)	O	O	◆	O	O	O	O	O	O	O	O	O	O	O	O	O	O	O	O	O	O	
In the Name of the Law (1)	O	O	O	O	O	O	O	O	O	O	O	O	O	O	O	O	O	O	O	O	O	
It's a Date (1)	O	O	O	O	O	O	O	O	O	O	O	O	O	O	O	O	O	O	O	O	O	
Once Upon a Time (2)	O	O	O	O	O	O	O	O	O	O	O	O	O	O	O	O	O	O	O	O	O	
Puzzled? (3)	O	O	O	O	O	O	O	O	O	O	O	O	O	O	O	O	O	O	O	O	O	
Rags to Stitches (1)	O	O	O	O	O	O	O	O	O	O	O	O	O	O	O	O	O	O	O	O	O	
Study Up! (3)	O	O	O	O	O	O	O	O	O	O	O	O	O	O	O	O	O	O	O	O	O	
Tongue Tied (4)	O	O	O	O	O	O	O	O	O	O	O	O	O	O	O	O	*	O	O	O	O	
Treble Trouble (2)	O	O	O	O	O	O	O	O	O	O	O	O	O	O	O	O	O	O	O	O	O	
Very Funny! (2)	O	*	*	O	*	O	O	O	O	O	O	O	O	O	O	O	*	O	O	O	O	
Other																						

Individual Activities:
Pencil, Marker, & Paper Activity Starters

	1	2	3	4	5	6	7	8	9	10	11	12	13	14	15	16	17	18	19	20	21	22
About Face (1)	O	O	O	O	O	O	O	O	O	O	O	O	O	O	O	O	O	O	O	O	O	
Greetings! (1)	O	O	O	O	O	O	O	O	O	O	O	O	O	O	O	O	*	O	O	O	O	
Hang Ups (1)	O	O	O	O	O	O	O	O	O	O	O	O	O	O	O	O	O	O	O	O	O	
Hats Off to You (1)	O	O	O	O	O	O	O	O	O	O	O	O	O	O	O	O	O	O	O	O	O	
Papier Trained (1)	O	O	O	O	O	O	O	O	O	O	O	O	O	O	O	O	O	O	O	O	O	
Say "Cheese" (1)	O	O	O	O	O	O	O	O	O	O	O	O	O	O	O	O	O	O	O	O	O	
Other																						

Partner and Group Activities

All "Partner and Group Activities" combinations work well together; thus, no grid is included.

○ Excellent combination

◆ Good combination (needs minor rewording)

* Teacher discretion advised

CURRICULUM AREA: PROFESSIONALLY SPEAKING: JEWISH CAREERS

Suggested Topics:

1. The Rabbi's first pulpit.

2. A tone-deaf cantor.

3. A religious school director's retirement speech.

4. A religious school teacher's greatest task.

5. A special delivery for the curator of a Jewish museum.

6. A dilemma for the director of the U.J.A. (or HIAS or another Jewish organization).

7. Being a tour director in Israel.

8. Working at a Jewish home for the elderly (or a Jewish children's home, Jewish hospital, etc.).

9. The most important thing about a J.C.C. (or YW/YMHA) director.

10. The goals of a Jewish social worker.

11. Recommendations of a kosher restaurant.

12. The thoughts of a new <u>mohel</u>.

13. A *<u>sofer's</u>* special training.

14. An ethical concern of the publisher of a Jewish newspaper.

15. The ordering practices of the owner of a Jewish bookstore orgift shop.

16. The job of a *<u>shochet</u>* or a kosher butcher.

17. A <u>Dayan</u>'s most difficult case.

18. Other:

Individual Activities:
Pencil, Marker, & Paper Activity Starters

	1	2	3	4	5	6	7	8	9	10	11	12	13	14	15	16	17	18	19
And I Quote (2)	○	○	○	○	○	○	○	○	○	○	○	○	○	○	○	○	○	○	
Attention, Please (1)	○	○	○	○	○	○	○	○	○	○	○	○	○	○	○	○	○	○	
Dear Diary (3)	○	○	○	○	○	○	○	○	○	○	○	○	○	○	○	○	○	○	
Extra! Extra! (1)	○	○	○	○	○	○	○	○	○	○	○	○	○	○	○	○	○	○	
Haiku! (Gesundheit!) (1)	○	○	○	○	○	○	○	○	○	○	○	○	○	○	○	○	○	○	
Hold the Presses (2)	○	○	○	○	○	○	○	○	○	○	○	○	○	○	○	○	○	○	
In the Name of the Law (1)	○	○	○	○	○	○	○	○	○	○	○	○	○	○	○	○	○	○	
It's a Date (1)	○	○	○	○	○	○	○	○	○	○	○	○	○	○	○	○	○	○	
Once Upon a Time (2)	○	○	○	○	○	○	○	○	○	○	○	○	○	○	○	○	○	○	
Puzzled? (3)	○	○	○	○	○	○	○	○	○	○	○	○	○	○	○	○	○	○	
Rags to Stitches (1)	○	○	○	○	○	○	○	○	○	○	○	○	○	○	○	○	○	○	
Study Up! (3)	○	○	○	○	○	○	○	○	○	○	○	○	○	○	○	○	○	○	
Tongue Tied (4)	○	○	○	○	○	○	○	○	○	○	○	○	○	○	○	○	○	○	
Treble Trouble (2)	○	○	○	○	○	○	○	○	○	○	○	○	○	○	○	○	○	○	
Very Funny! (2)	○	○	○	○	○	○	○	○	○	○	○	○	○	○	○	○	○	○	
Other																			

Individual Activities:
Pencil, Marker, & Paper Activity Starters

	1	2	3	4	5	6	7	8	9	10	11	12	13	14	15	16	17	18	19
About Face (1)	○	○	○	○	○	○	○	○	○	○	○	○	○	○	○	○	○	○	
Greetings! (1)	○	○	○	○	○	○	○	○	○	○	○	○	○	○	○	○	○	○	
Hang Ups (1)	○	○	○	○	○	○	○	○	○	○	○	○	○	○	○	○	○	○	
Hats Off to You (1)	○	○	○	○	○	○	○	○	○	○	○	○	○	○	○	○	○	○	
Papier Trained (1)	○	○	○	○	○	○	○	○	○	○	○	○	○	○	○	○	○	○	
Say "Cheese" (1)	○	○	○	○	○	○	○	○	○	○	○	○	○	○	○	○	○	○	
Other																			

Partner and Group Activities

All "Partner and Group Activities" combinations work well together; thus, no grid is included.

○   Excellent combination

◆   Good combination (needs minor rewording)

✳   Teacher discretion advised

GLOSSARY

ALIYAH – "going up." "Making *Aliyah*" and "going on *Aliyah*" are terms which mean immigrating to Israel.

BABYLONIAN TALMUD – the combination of the Mishna (see "Mishna") and Babylonian Gemara (one of two major interpretations of and elaborations upon the Mishna).

BALFOUR DECLARATION – a document issued by the British government in 1917 that supported the establishment of a Jewish homeland in Palestine.

BAR MITZVAH – "Son of the Commandment," a ceremony which signals a boy's passage from childhood to the age of religious responsibility, usually at age 13.

BAT MITZVAH – "Daughter of the Commandment," a ceremony which signals a girl's passage from childhood to the age of religious responsibility, usually at age 12 1/2.

BEN-GURION, DAVID (1886-1973) – first Prime Minister of Israel, proclaimed the establishment of the State of Israel in 1948.

BETA YISRAEL – "House of Israel," refers to the Jews of Ethiopia.

BRIT BAT – "Covenant of the Daughter," a naming ceremony which welcomes baby girls into Jewish life.

BRIT CHAYIM – "Covenant of Life," a naming ceremony which welcomes baby girls into Jewish life.

BRIT MILAH (BRIS) – "Covenant of Circumcision," a ceremony during which an eight-day-old Jewish boy is circumcised.

CANAAN, LAND OF – the name of the Land of Israel before the era of the kings of Israel.

CHABAD LUBAVITCH – a movement based on Hasidic philosophy (see "Hasidic Movement"). The letters in the word "Chabad" stand for *Chochma* (wisdom), *Binoh* (understanding), and *Da'as* (knowledge). Lubavitch is the name of the city where the Chabad movement was centered for many years. "Chabad" and "Lubavitch" are sometimes used interchangeably.

CHANUKAT HABAYIT – a ceremony during which the *mezzuzah* is affixed and a Jewish home is blessed.

CONFIRMATION – a ceremony which marks the completion of religious school (and the affirmation of one's commitment to the Jewish heritage).

CONSECRATION – a ceremony that signals the beginning of a child's formal religious education.

CONSERVATIVE JUDAISM – a branch of Judaism which began in Germany and America during the nineteenth century. A main tenet is that *halachah* (Jewish law) may be interpreted through consensus of the leaders of the movement.

DAVENING – praying.

DAYAN – a judge who serves on a Jewish religious court.

DEAD SEA SCROLLS – manuscripts probably written in the first century C.E. and uncovered in the twentieth century in caves near the Dead Sea.

DIASPORA – from the Greek word for "dispersion," refers to any and all Jewish communities outside of Israel.

HAGANAH – means "defense," the unofficial Jewish army in Palestine prior to the establishment of the State of Israel.

HASIDIC MOVEMENT – a branch of traditional Judaism founded by the Baal Shem Tov in the 1700s.

KAVANAH – heartfelt prayer.

KIBBUTZNIK – one who lives on a *kibbutz*, an Israeli settlement where the property and chores are shared by all of the members.

KNESSET – the Israeli parliament.

KOTEL HAMA'ARAV – "Western Wall," a last retaining wall from the Holy Temple in Jerusalem; the holiest Jewish site. Also called *HaKotel* (the Wall).

MAGEN DAVID – means "shield of David" and usually refers to the six pointed star.

MAMA-LOSHEN – "mother tongue," usually refers to Yiddish.

MARRANO – Jews from Spain who practiced their religion in secret.

MEGILLAT ESTHER – "Scroll of Esther," the story of Esther read on Purim.

MEIR, GOLDA (1898-1978) – Israel's fourth Prime Minister.

MEZZUZAH – parchment on which the *Sh'ma* and *Ve'ahavta* are written. The *Mezzuzah* is placed on the doorposts of Jewish homes.

MISHNA – a collection of laws written by the Sages over a period of three centuries. It was codified by Judah HaNasi in approximately 200 C.E.

MIZRACH – means "east," specifically, a plaque or weaving placed on the east wall of a home or synagogue to indicate the direction to face in prayer.

MOHEL – a person specially trained to perform ritual circumcision.

OPERATION MOSES – a secret airlift which brought 8,000 Jewish Ethiopian refugees to Israel between November of 1984 and January of 1985.

ORTHODOX JUDAISM – a branch of Judaism which posits strict adherence to Jewish customs and traditions and to the principles of *halachah* (Jewish law).

PIRKE AVOT (ETHICS OF THE FATHERS) – a tractate of the Mishna which contains aphorisms and value statements to guide us in our daily conduct.

PIDYON HA-BEN – means "Redemption of the Firstborn." In biblical times, an Israelite son who was the firstborn of his mother was to serve as a priest unless his father bought him back (redeemed him) from this duty. Today, this practice of redeeming the firstborn is still performed on the 31st day of life.

RABBENU GERSHOM – a Talmudic scholar who lived around 1000 C.E. Referred to as "the Light of the Exile," Rabbenu Gershom authored many *Takanot* (Rabbinic decisions) and influenced another famous scholar, Rashi (see "Rashi").

RASHI (1040-1105) – a French Rabbi and scholar whose commentaries on the Talmud and Bible are most significant.

RECONSTRUCTIONIST JUDAISM – a branch of Judaism founded in the 1920s by Rabbi Mordecai Kaplan, who taught that Jews are a people and that Judaism is a civilization consisting of language, customs, traditions, history, and religion.

REFORM JUDAISM – a branch of Judaism that began in Germany in the early nineteenth century and was founded in America by Rabbi Isaac Mayer Wise. Rooted in the prophetic teachings, Reform Jews are encouraged to make educated choices regarding personal religious practices.

SIMCHAT HA-BAT – "Rejoicing of the Daughter," a naming ceremony which welcomes female babies into Jewish life.

SHOCHET – a person trained to perform the slaughter of animals according to the laws of *kashrut*.

SOFER – a scribe who writes Torah scrolls, *mezzuzot*, and *tefillin*.

SUKKAH – a temporary booth constructed for the harvest festival Sukkot.

TEFILLIN – "phylacteries," two small boxes, one to be worn on the forehead and the other on the arm during morning prayers.

TZEDAKAH – "righteousness," usually refers to acts of good deeds and charity.

WEIZMANN, CHAIM (1874-1952) – a Zionist leader who became the first President of Israel in 1948.

YAHRZEIT – the anniversary of a death.

BEYOND 10,000

Need more activity ideas? Here are suggestions from A to Z . . . almost.

A dvertisements

B ulletin board displays

C ollages

D efinitions

E ulogies

F lags

G raphs

H appenings and events

I nventions

J ingles

K its

L ectures

M odels

N eedlework

O rigami

P lans

Q uotations

R eenactments

S hadow boxes

T rials

W arnings

Y ellow Pages

REFERENCES

Many fine sources were tapped in the course of preparing *The Teacher Pleaser*. Among those books included during the research process were the following:

Burstein, Chaya M. *The Jewish Kids Catalog*. Philadelphia: The Jewish Publication Society of America, 1983.

Charing, Douglas. *The Jewish World*. Morristown, NJ: Silver Burdett Company, 1983.

Jones, Helen Hinckley. *Enchantment of the World – Israel*. Chicago: Children's Press, 1986.

Kubie, Nora Benjamin. *Israel*. New York: Franklin Watts, 1978.

Scharfstein, Sol. *Let's Learn Prayer*. Hoboken, NJ: KTAV Publishing House, Inc., 1985.

Zohar, Danah. *Israel: The Land and Its People*. Morristown, NJ: Silver Burdette Company, 1977.